AuthorHouse™ UK Ltd.
500 Avebury Boulevard
Central Milton Keynes, MK9 2BE
www.authorhouse.co.uk
Phone: 08001974150

First published by AuthorHouse   5/12/2011

ISBN: 978-1-4567-7627-5 (sc)

This book is printed on acid-free paper.

TAEKWON-DO

POOMSE

MADE EASY!

CONTENTS

ACKNOWLEDGEMENTS:

I would like to thank all my trainers:

- My first trainer - Master Kwok Wan, 7th Dan WTF (London)
- My 1st Dan - Master Shin Jang Hwan, 9th Dan WTF (Vienna)
- My 2nd Dan - Master Yoon Dongil, 6th Dan WTF (Vienna)
- My 3rd and 4th Dan - Master Nobert Mosch (Dr.), 8th Dan WTF (Vienna)

Hana

Dul

Set

Net

Dasot

Yasot

Ilgub

Yodol

Ahob

Yol

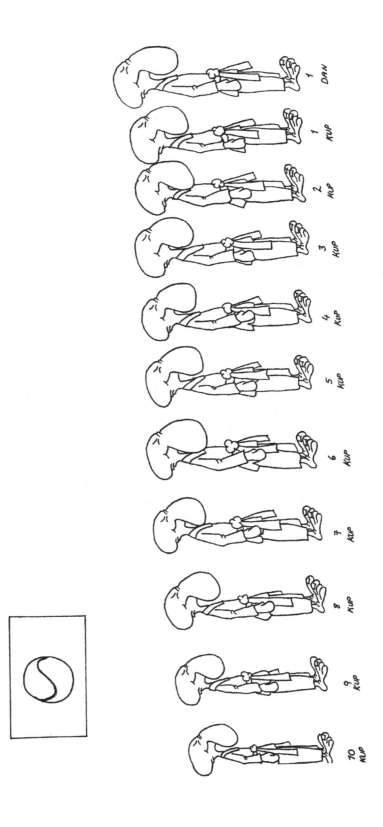

PROLOGUE

Once upon a time, not so long ago, in a land far far away in Africa, a Bug was born. The Bug grew up in the Sahara desert, and by the age of three was an experienced and very talented hunter.

The Bug used to hunt for insects and wild animals, including donkeys, to sell for cash to the meat processing factory in the capital Khartoum. One day the Bug made a good catch of three donkeys and various insects, and so travelled down to the city to make business. While in the capital, the Bug stopped at a local restaurant to eat some vegetables. The Bug watched a program, on TV, about Australia which showed very nice pictures of a very strange type of animal called a Koala. For Bug it was love at first sight and it decided to get such an animal to keep as a pet.

The Bug decided to travel to Australia, so it went back to the desert to collect its belongings. It packed three insects, a stick and a comb and went to the nearest airport. On its way to Australia the Bug landed in Austria where it wanted to stay for a few days to visit some friends.

While in Austria, the Bug received a letter of invitation from some strange friends in Germany. The Bug went to see its friends. "I am going to study at London University" said one of the strange friends. So the Bug made up its mind to go to England, instead of Australia, and become an intellectual. Now England is not very far from Germany, so in no time the Bug arrived in England and enrolled as a student at the University of London. One day, the Bug went to look at the University sports Institute; it wanted to pick up squash to keep fit. However, when it got there, it found a lot of people dressed in white pyjamas with different ropes round the middle.

The Bug wondered what they were doing at the sports facility. After a while, the Master came into the gym, and all the people lined up just like in the army. It then saw something very rare indeed, the master, who was not very big, could do all sorts of incredible things. He could kick very high, he could punch very hard, he could jump in the air and he could kick from behind. He could break wood and he could jump and kick at the same time. Not only this, he could kick in all directions from all positions at the same time and he could see from behind the back of his head!!!

The bug knew that it had found a very strange thing indeed. It said to the Master "I WANT!! I WANT!!". The Master replied "Yes, but not before you learn your poomse 1,2,3….."

TAEKWONDO AN INTRODUCTION

Taekwondo is an ancient Korean martial art dating back to about 50 BC. Translated, Tae means to kick (foot technique), Kwon means to punch (hand technique) and Do means discipline or art. In Taekwondo, powerful and varied kicking techniques are emphasized; which distinguishes it from other martial art forms. The discipline of Taekwondo comprises speed, endurance and technique which are achieved through proper training. It incorporates both straight line and flowing circular movements.

Historically Taekwondo originated as a martial art and a form of self defence in unarmed combat at the time when Korea was divided into three Kingdoms: Silla, Kyongju and Koguryo. Taekwondo first appeared in the Koguryo Kingdom (37 B.C.~668 A.D) where elite members called Sun Bae were dedicated warriors. However it was Silla's warrior nobility (57 A.D~935 A.D) the Hwa Rang who were responsible for the spread of Taekwondo. The Hwa Rang Do was a military, educational and social organization. During the koryo dynasty (935 A.D.~1392 A.D.) Taek Kyon became known as Subak and developed into a predominantly fighting art and techniques were refined and improved.

During the Yi dynasty (1393 A.D.~1910 A.D) the practice of martial arts was not encouraged but a large number of common people still continued to practice the techniques of Korean martial arts. During the Japanese occupation of Korea (1910-1945) all Korean cultural activity including the practice of Korean martial arts was prohibited. When Korea gained independence in 1945, and after the end of the Korean War (1950~1953), cultural and social aspects began to return to normal and Taekwondo techniques began to improve.

Modern Taekwondo:

Originally different names were used to describe Taekwondo including Taek Gyeon, Soo Bak Do, Kong Soo Do, Tang Soo Do and others. In 1961 the Tae Soo Do association was formed, which in 1965 changed their name to the Korean Tae Kwon Do Association. The first leaders of the Korean Taekwondo Association used their authority and sent instructors and demonstration teams all over the world, spreading the art to every continent. In 1973 the World Taekwondo Federation (WTF) was established. Since then, many national and international sporting bodies entered Taekwondo as an event in their games. Examples include the International Sports Federation, the International Military Sports Council, the Pan American Sports Organization, the Asian games and the Olympic Committee. In 1988 Taekwondo was included in the Olympics as an exhibition sport. In 1994 it was accepted as an official Olympic sport by the International Olympic Committee (IOC) and was included for the first time in the 2000 Olympiad in Sydney, Australia.

POOMSE

Poomse is a prearranged series of attack and defense movements against an imaginary opponent in a set pattern. For each belt grading or next level of advancement the Taekwondo student must be able to master the poomse for that level.

The practice of poomse improves breathing and physical control, strength, coordination, timing and balance. It also increases internal strength by conditioning the internal organs and the student masters the ability to use different types of power including stationary or sudden bursts (momentary power). It uses both flowing as well as quick abrupt movements. The primary forms of Taekwondo are known as the Tae Geuk series. Literally translated Tae Geuk means great eternity. The first eight patterns of the Tae Geuk series derive their meanings from the oriental philosophical views and include the theory of Yin and Yang (negative and positive). Each of the primary patterns (1-8) is symbolized by a different element:

- Heaven and universe -Yang (Keon) – Il Jang
- Inner firmness and outer softness (Tae) – E Jang
- Hot and bright (Yi) Sam Jang
- Thunder (Jin) – Sa Jan
- Wind (Seon) – Oh Jang
- Water (Kam) – Yuk Jang
- Mountain (Kan) – Chil Jang
- Earth-Yin (Kon) – Pal Jang

The second eight patterns of the series starts with Koryo (black belt pattern) and represent little stories in Korean history. The symbol of Tae Geuk is shown below (historical symbol shown on the left). The two parts in the circle represent Yin and Yang in a rotating form.

SOME STANCES

Naranhi-Seogi
(Parallel stance)

Moa-Seogi
(Closed stance)

Pyonhi-Seogi
(At ease
stance)

Dwichuk-Moa-
Seogi (Attention
stance)

Juchum-Seogi
(Horse riding
stance)

Ap-Seogi
(Walking stance)

Ap-Kubi
(Long stance)

Dwitkubi
(Back stance)

Beom-Seogi
(Tiger stance)

Kkoa-Seogi
(Twist stance)

Oen-Seogi
(Left hand stance)

Oreun-Seogi (Right hand stance)

Hakdari-Seogi
(Crane stance)

10

SOME BLOCKS

Arae-Makki
(Low section block)

Olgul-Makki
(High section
block)

Anmakki
(Inner section
block)

Sonnal-Mok-
Chigi
(Knife hand
strike)

Hansonal-
Momtong-bakkat-
Makki
(Knife hand
middle section
block)

Sonal-Momtong-
Makki
(Double knife hand
block)

Bakkat-Makki
(Outer arm block)

Deung-Jumok-
Ap-Chigi
(Back fist strike)

Mejumok-
Naeryo-Chigi
(Back fist
strike)

Palgup-Dollyo-
Chigi
(Elbow strike)

Batangson-Momtong
-Anmakki
(Middle section palm
block)

Geodeureo-Makki
(Double block)

Momtong-Baro -
Jireugi
(Middle section
punch)

Arae-Hechyo-Makki
(X Double lower section blocks)

11

TAEGUK EL JANG

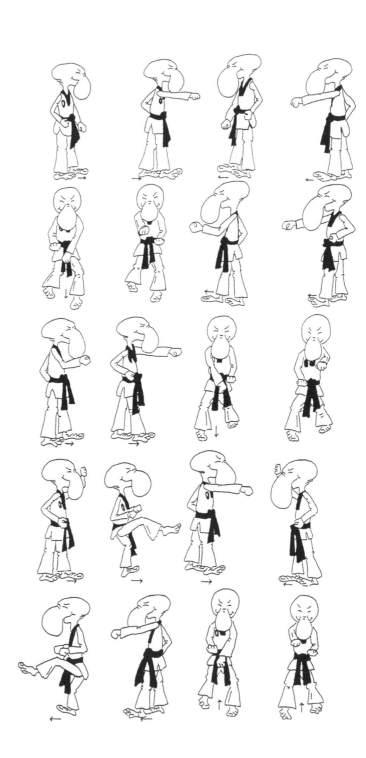

"BUG, 1995"

TAEGUK 1 Jang

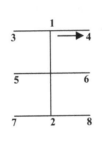

Pivoting on the right foot, turn 90° to the left (direction 4), into a left walking stance (apseogi) and exectue a lower section block with the left arm (arae-makki).

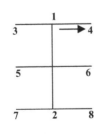

Moving in the same direction (4), step forward with the right foot into a right walking stance (apseogi) and execute a middle section reverse punch with the right fist (momtong-bandae-jireugi).

13

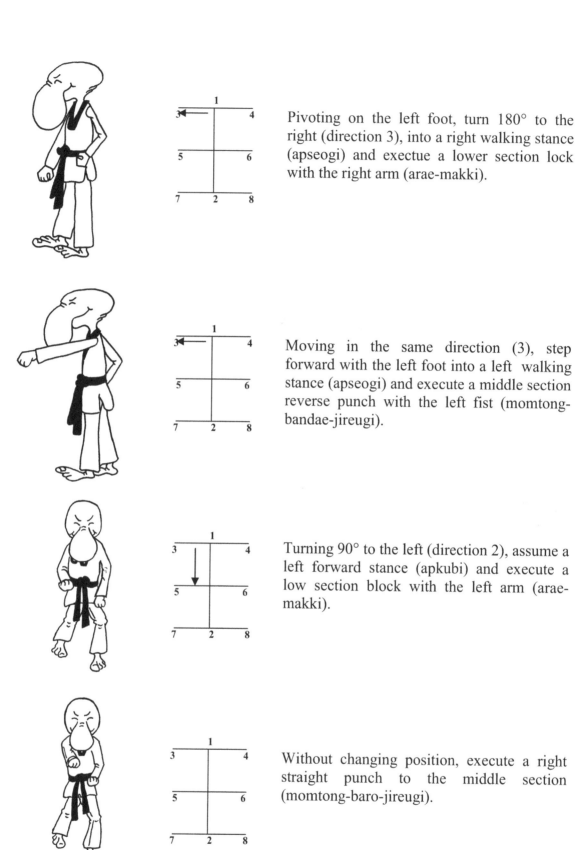

Pivoting on the left foot, turn 180° to the right (direction 3), into a right walking stance (apseogi) and exectue a lower section lock with the right arm (arae-makki).

Moving in the same direction (3), step forward with the left foot into a left walking stance (apseogi) and execute a middle section reverse punch with the left fist (momtong-bandae-jireugi).

Turning 90° to the left (direction 2), assume a left forward stance (apkubi) and execute a low section block with the left arm (arae-makki).

Without changing position, execute a right straight punch to the middle section (momtong-baro-jireugi).

14

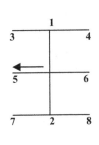

Pivoting on the left foot turn 90° to the right (direction 5), and assume a right walking stance (apseogi). At the same time execute a middle section inside block (from out to in) with the left arm (momtong-anmakki).

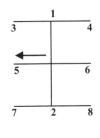

Moving in the same direction (5), step forward with the left foot into a left walking stance (apseogi) and execute a right straight punch to the middle section (momtong-baro-jireugi).

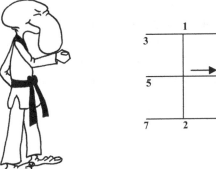

Pivoting on the right foot turn 180° to the left (direction 6), and assume a left walking stance (apseogi). At the same time execute a middle section inside block (from out to in) with the right arm (momtong-anmakki).

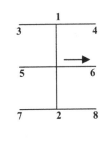

Moving in the same direction (6), step forward with the right foot into a right walking stance (apseogi) and execute a left straight punch to the middle section (momtong-baro-jireugi).

15

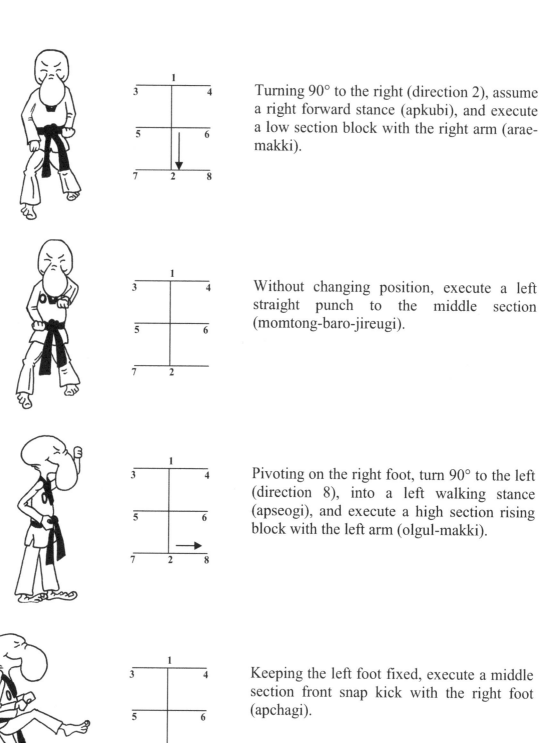

Turning 90° to the right (direction 2), assume a right forward stance (apkubi), and execute a low section block with the right arm (arae-makki).

Without changing position, execute a left straight punch to the middle section (momtong-baro-jireugi).

Pivoting on the right foot, turn 90° to the left (direction 8), into a left walking stance (apseogi), and execute a high section rising block with the left arm (olgul-makki).

Keeping the left foot fixed, execute a middle section front snap kick with the right foot (apchagi).

16

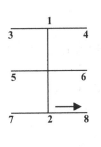

Step down into a right walking stance (direction 8, apseogi), and execute a middle section reverse punch with the right fist (momtong-bandae-jireugi).

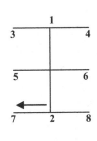

Pivoting on the left foot, turn 180° to the right (direction 7), into a right walking stance (apseogi), and execute a high section rising block with the right arm (olgul-makki).

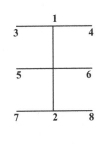

Keeping the right foot fixed, execute a middle section front snap kick with the left foot (apchagi).

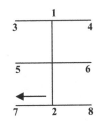

Step down into a left walking stance (direction 7, apseogi), and execute a middle section reverse punch with the left fist (momtong-bandae-jireugi).

 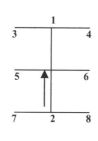

Pivoting on the right foot, turn 90° to the right (direction 1), into a left forward stance (apkubi) and execute a low section block with the left arm (arae-makki).

 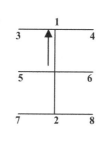

Step forward with the right foot into a right forward stance (apkubi) and execute a right middle section reverse punch (momtong-bandae-jireugi).

KIHAPP!

TAEGUK E JANG

"BUG, 1995"

© Salma
Michor, VBK,
Vienna

19

TAEGUK 2 Jang

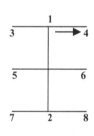

Pivoting on the right foot, turn 90° to the left into a left walking stance (apseogi, direction 4) and execute a left low section block (arae-makki).

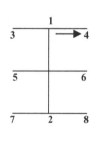

Keeping the left foot fixed, step forward with the right foot into a right forward stance (apkubi, direction 4), and execute a right middle section reverse puch (momtong-bandae-jireugi).

 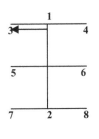 Pivoting on the left foot, turn 180° to the right into a right walking stance (apseogi, direction 3) and execute a right low section block (arae-makki).

 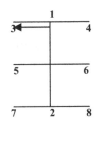 Keeping the right foot fixed, step forward with the left foot into a left forward stance (apkubi, direction 3), and execute a left middle section reverse puch (momtong-bandae-jireugi).

 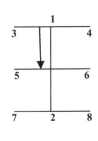 Pivoting on the right foot, turn 90° to the left into a left walking stance (apseogi, facing 2), and execute a right middle section inside block (from out to in, momtong-anmakki).

 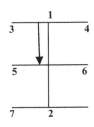 Stepping forward with the right foot in the same direction (2), assume a right walking stance (apseogi), and execute a left middle section inside block (from out to in, momtong-anmakki).

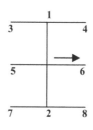

Pivoting on the right foot, turn 90° to the left into a left walking stance (apseogi, direction 6) and execute a left low section block (arae-makki).

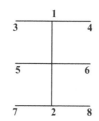

Keeping the left foot fixed, execute a right front snap kick (apchagi).

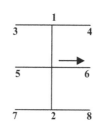

Step down with the right foot into a right forward stance (apkubi) and execute a right high section reverse punch (olgul-bandae-jireugi).

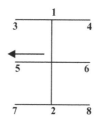

Pivoting on the left foot, turn 180° to the right into a right walking stance (apseogi, direction 5), and execute a right low section block (arae-makki).

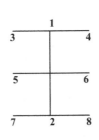

Keeping the right foot fixed, execute a left front snap kick (apchagi).

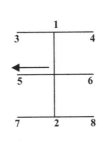

Step down with the left foot into a left forward stance (apkubi) and execute a right high section reverse punch (olgul-bandae-jireugi).

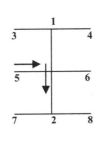

Pivoting on the right foot, turn 90° to the left into a left walking stance (apseogi, facing 2), and execute a left high section rising block (olgul-makki).

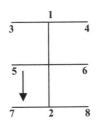

Keeping the left foot fixed, step forward with the right foot into a right walking stance (apseogi), and execute a right high section rising block (olgul-makki).

23

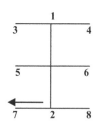

Pivoting on the right foot, turn 270° to the left into a left walking stance (apseogi, direction 7), and execute an inside middle section block (from out to in, momtong-anmakki) with the right arm.

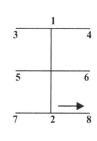

Pivoting on the left foot, turn 180° to the right into a right walking stance (apseogi, direction 8), and execute an inside middle section block (from out to in, momtong-anmakki) with the left arm.

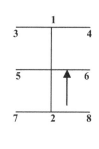

Pivoting on the right foot, turn 90° to the left into a left walking stance (apseogi, direction 1), and execute a low section block with the left arm (arae-makki).

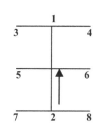

Keeping the left foot fixed, execute a front snap kick, with the right foot (apchagi).

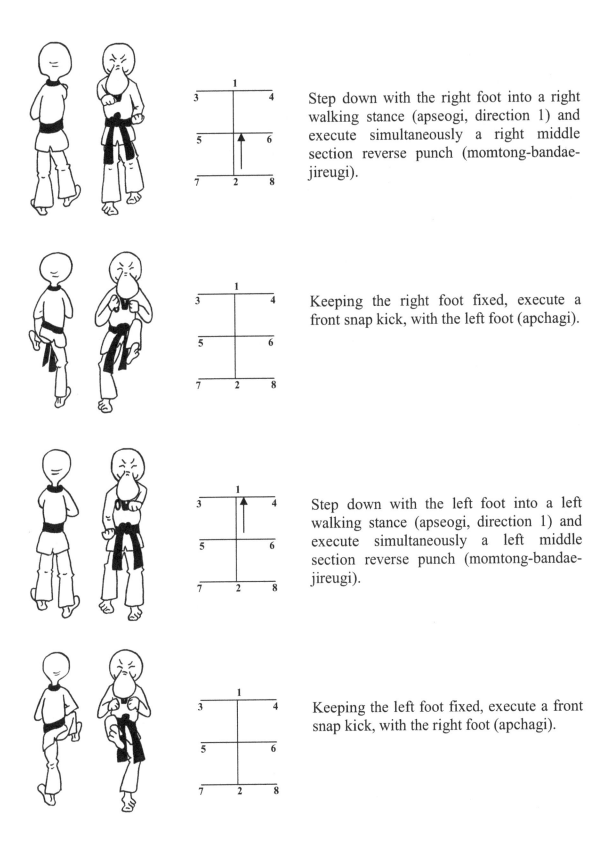

Step down with the right foot into a right walking stance (apseogi, direction 1) and execute simultaneously a right middle section reverse punch (momtong-bandae-jireugi).

Keeping the right foot fixed, execute a front snap kick, with the left foot (apchagi).

Step down with the left foot into a left walking stance (apseogi, direction 1) and execute simultaneously a left middle section reverse punch (momtong-bandae-jireugi).

Keeping the left foot fixed, execute a front snap kick, with the right foot (apchagi).

25

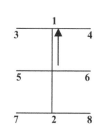

```
        1
3  ┌─────▲─────┐  4
   │     │     │
5  ├─────┼─────┤  6
   │     │     │
7  └─────┼─────┘  8
   7     2     8
```

Step down with the right foot into a right walking stance (apseogi, direction 1), and execute a right middle section reverse punch (momtong-bandae-jireugi).

KIHAPP!

26

TAEGUK SAM JANG

"BUG, 1995"

© Salma Michor, VBK, Vienna

TAEGUK 3 Jang

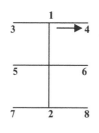

Pivoting on the right foot, turn 90° to the left into a left walking stance (apseogi, direction 4), and exectue a low section block with the left arm (arae-makki).

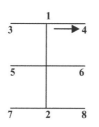

Keeping the left foot fixed, execute a right front snap kick (apchagi).

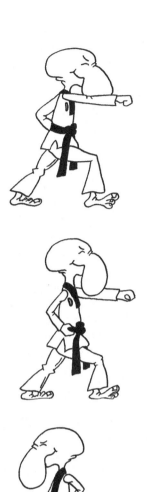

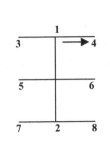

Stepping down with the right foot into a right forward stance (apkubi), execute a right …

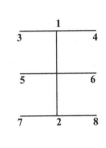

… then a left middle section straight punch in rapid succession (momtong-dubeon-jireugi).

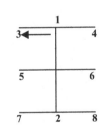

Pivoting on the left foot, turn 180° to the right into a right walking stance (apseogi, direction 3), and exectue a low section block with the right arm (arae-makki).

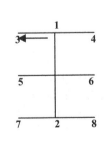

Keeping the right foot fixed, execute a left front snap kick (apchagi).

29

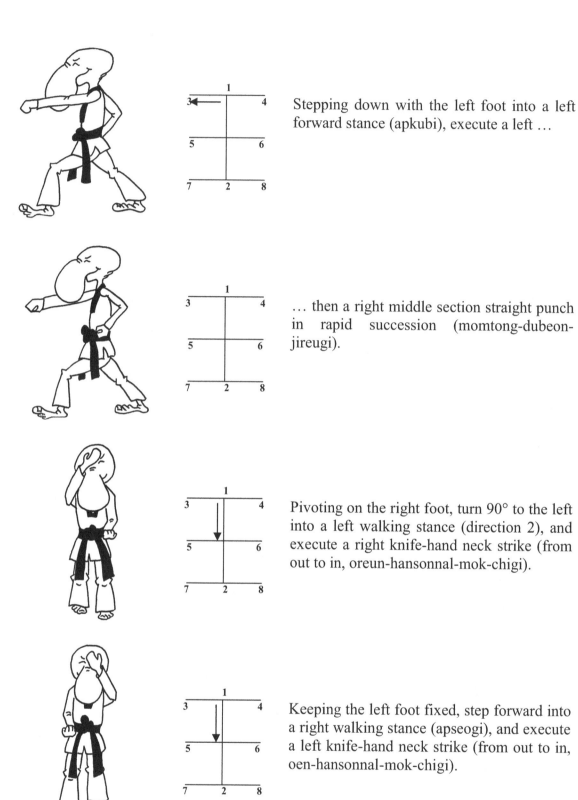

Stepping down with the left foot into a left forward stance (apkubi), execute a left …

… then a right middle section straight punch in rapid succession (momtong-dubeon-jireugi).

Pivoting on the right foot, turn 90° to the left into a left walking stance (direction 2), and execute a right knife-hand neck strike (from out to in, oreun-hansonnal-mok-chigi).

Keeping the left foot fixed, step forward into a right walking stance (apseogi), and execute a left knife-hand neck strike (from out to in, oen-hansonnal-mok-chigi).

Keeping the right foot fixed, turn 90° to the left and assume a right back stance (oreun-dwitkubi, direction 6). At the same time execute a left knife-hand middle section block (from in to out, oen-hansonnal-momtong-bakkat-makki).

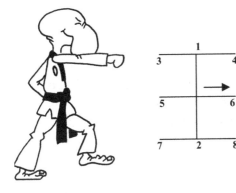

Slide forward with the left foot into a left forward stance (apkubi, direction 6), and execute a right middle section straight punch (momtong-baro-jireugi).

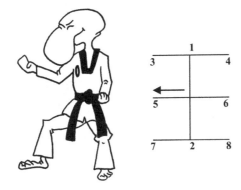

Pivoting on the left foot, turn 180° to the right (direction 5), and assume a left back stance (oen-dwitkubi). At the same time execute a right knife-hand middle section block (from in to out, oreun-hansonnal-momtong-bakkat-makki).

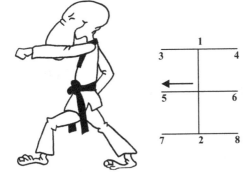

Slide forward with the right foot into a right forward stance (apkubi, direction 5), and execute a left middle section straight punch (momtong-baro-jireugi).

 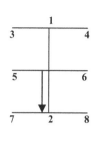

Pivoting on the right foot, turn 90° to the left into a left walking stance (apseogi, direction 2), and execute a right inward forearm block (middle section, momtong-anmakki).

 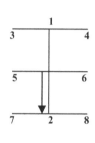

Keeping the left foot fixed, step forward with the right foot into a right walking stance (apseogi) and execute a left inward forearm block (momtong-anmakki).

 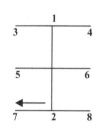

Pivoting on the right foot, turn 270° to the left (apseogi, direction 7), into a left walking stance and execute a low section block with the left arm (arae-makki).

 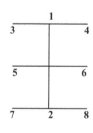

Keeping the left foot fixed, execute a right front snap kick (apchagi).

Stepping down with the right foot into a right forward stance (apkubi), execute a right …

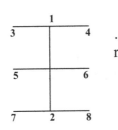

… then a left middle section straight punch in rapid succession (momtong-dubeon-jireugi).

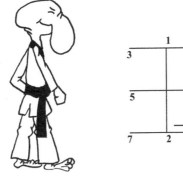

Pivoting on the left foot, turn 180° to the right (apseogi, direction 8), into a right walking stance and execute a low section block with the right arm (arae-makki).

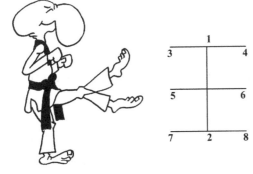

Keeping the right foot fixed, execute a left front snap kick (apchagi).

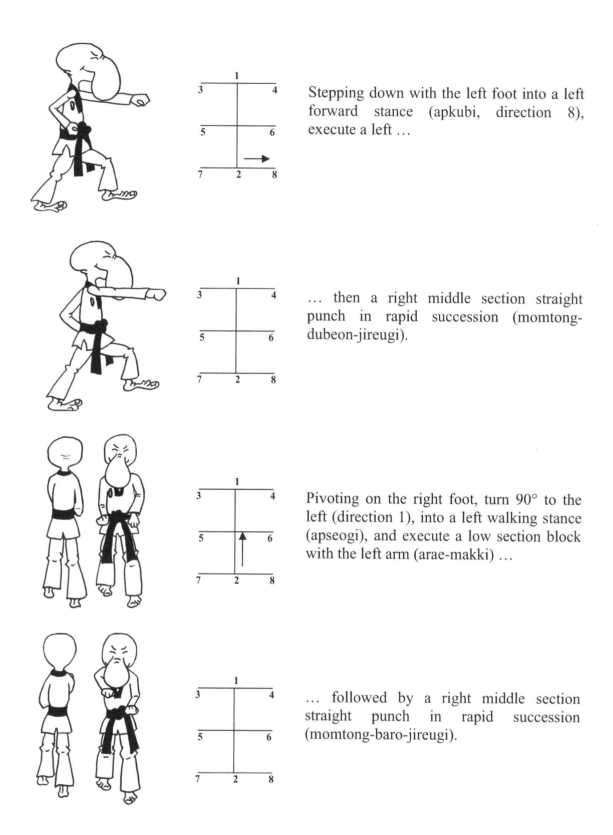

Stepping down with the left foot into a left forward stance (apkubi, direction 8), execute a left …

… then a right middle section straight punch in rapid succession (momtong-dubeon-jireugi).

Pivoting on the right foot, turn 90° to the left (direction 1), into a left walking stance (apseogi), and execute a low section block with the left arm (arae-makki) …

… followed by a right middle section straight punch in rapid succession (momtong-baro-jireugi).

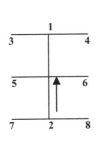

Keeping the left foot fixed, step forward into a right walking stance (apseogi, direction 1), and execute a right low section block (arae-makki)…

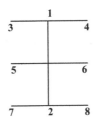

…followed by a left middle section straight punch in rapid succession (momtong-baro-jirugi).

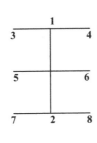

Keeping the right foot fixed, execute a left front snap kick (apchagi).

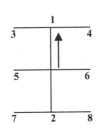

Stepping down into a left walking stance (apseogi), execute a left low section block (arae-makki) …

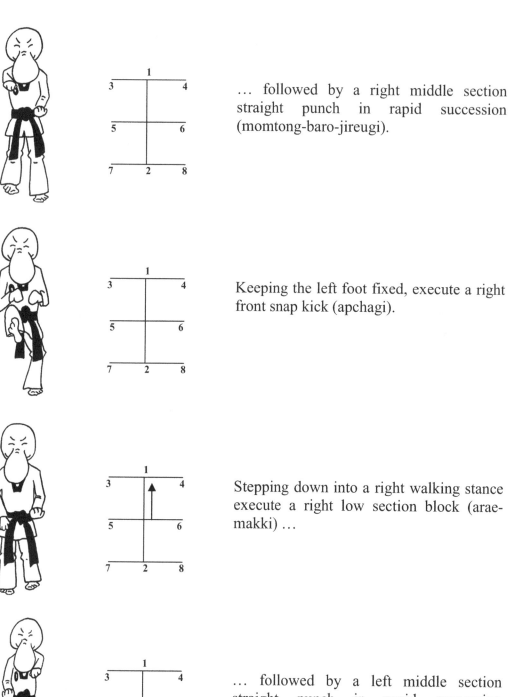

... followed by a right middle section straight punch in rapid succession (momtong-baro-jireugi).

Keeping the left foot fixed, execute a right front snap kick (apchagi).

Stepping down into a right walking stance execute a right low section block (arae-makki) ...

... followed by a left middle section straight punch in rapid succession (momtong-baro-jireugi).

KIHAPP!

T A E G U K   S A   J A N G

"BUG, 1995"

© Salma
Michor, VBK,
Vienna

TAEGUK 4 Jang

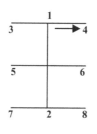

Keeping the right foot fixed, turn 90° to the left into a right back stance (oreun-dwitkubi, direction 4), and execute a double knife-hand block (sonnal-momting-makki).

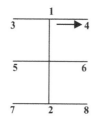

Keeping the left foot fixed, step forwad into a right forward stance (apkubi) while simultaneously executing a palm block with the left hand and a middle section spear hand strike with the right (nullo-makki and oreun-pyeonsonkeut-seweo-chireugi).

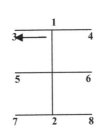

Pivoting on the left foot, turn 180° to the right (direction 3), into a left back stance (oen-dwitkubi) and execute a double knife-hand block (sonnal-momtong-makki).

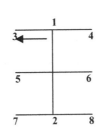

Keeping the right foot fixed, step forward into a left forward stance (apkubi) while simultaneoulsy executing a palm block with the right hand and a middle section spear hand strike with the left (nullo-makki and oen-pyeonsonkeut-seweo-chireugi).

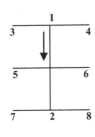

Pivoting on the right foot, turn 90° to the left, into a left forward stance (apkubi, direction 2). At the same time execute simultaneously a left knife-hand high section block and a right knife-hand neck strike (jebipum-mok-chigi).

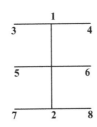

Keeping the left foot fixed, execute a right front snap kick (apchagi).

39

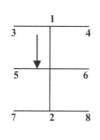

Step down with the right foot into a right forward stance (apkubi) and execute a left middle section straight punch (momtong-baro-jireugi).

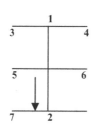

Pivoting on the right foot execute a left side kick (middle section, oen-yop-chagi).

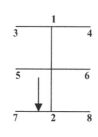

Stepping down with the left foot, pivot quickly and execute a right middle section side kick (oreun-yop-chagi).

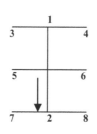

Step down into a left back stance (oen-dwitkubi) and execute a double knife-hand block (sonnal-momtong-makki).

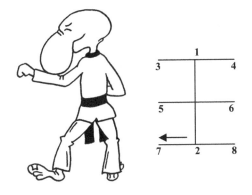

Pivoting on the right foot, turn 270° to the left into a right back stance (oreundwitkubi) and execute an outer arm middle section block with the left arm (from in to out, momtong-bakkat-makki).

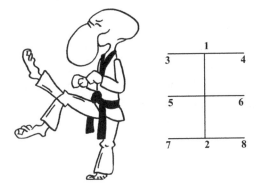

Execute a right front snap kick with the right foot (apchagi).

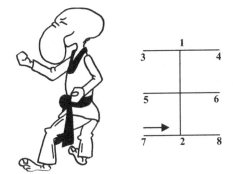

Step back into a right back stance (oreundwitkubi) while sliding with the left foot slightly backwards. At the same time execute a right middle section inner arm block (from out to in, momtong-anmakki).

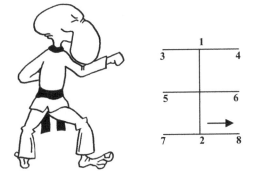

Pivoting on the left foot, turn 180° to the right (direction 8), into a left back stance (oen-dwitkubi) and execute an outer arm middle section block with the right arm (from in to out, momtong-bakkat-makki).

41

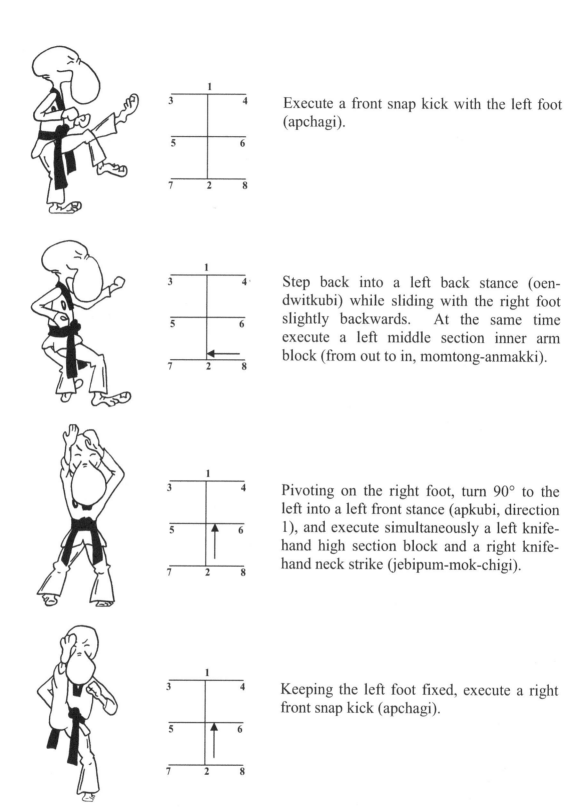

Execute a front snap kick with the left foot (apchagi).

Step back into a left back stance (oen-dwitkubi) while sliding with the right foot slightly backwards. At the same time execute a left middle section inner arm block (from out to in, momtong-anmakki).

Pivoting on the right foot, turn 90° to the left into a left front stance (apkubi, direction 1), and execute simultaneously a left knife-hand high section block and a right knife-hand neck strike (jebipum-mok-chigi).

Keeping the left foot fixed, execute a right front snap kick (apchagi).

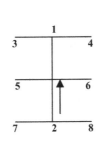

Step down into a right front stance (apkubi, direction 1), and execute a right back fist strike to the face (oreun-deungjumok-ap-chigi).

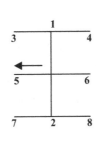

Pivoting on the right foot, turn 90° to the left (apseogi, direction 5), and execute a left middle section inside block (from out to in, momtong-makki).

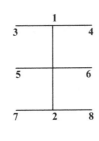

In the same position execute a right middle section straight punch (momtong-baro-jireugi).

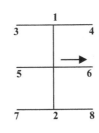

Pivoting on the left foot, turn 180° to the right into a right walking stance (apseogi, direction 6), and execute a right middle section inside block (from out to in, momtong-makki).

43

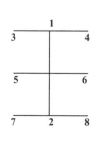

In the same position, execute a left middle section straight punch (momtong-baro-jireugi).

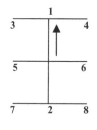

Pivoting on the right foot, turn 90° to the left (direction 1), into a left front stance (apkubi) and execute a left inner arm block (from out to in, momtong-makki).

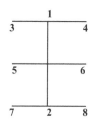

In the same position, execute a right …

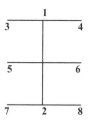

… then a left middle section punch in rapid succession (momtong-dubeon-jireugi).

44

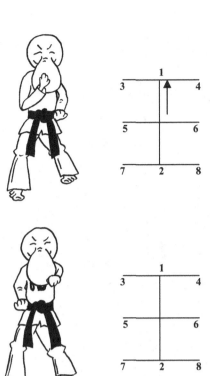

Step forward with the right foot into a right forward stance (apkubi, direction 1), and execute a right inner arm block (from out to in, momtong-makki).

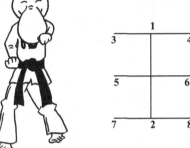

In the same position, execute a left ...

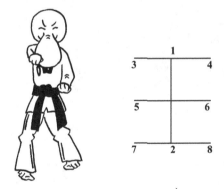

... then a right middle section punch in rapid succession (momtong-dubeon-jireugi).

KIHAPP!

TAEGUK OH JANG

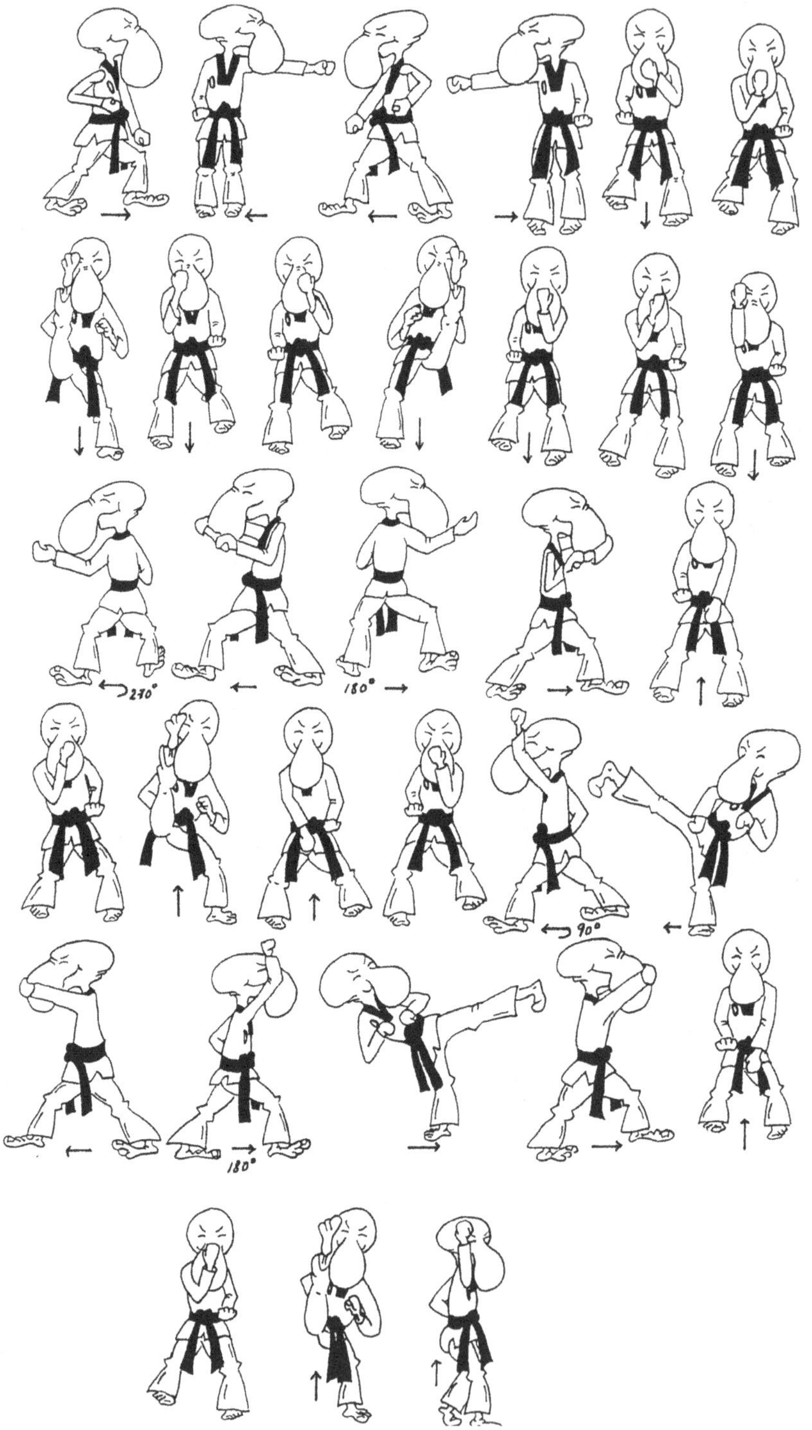

"BUG, 1995"

© Salma
Michor,
VBK,
Vienna

TAEGUK 5 Jang

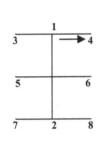

Pivoting on the rigth foot, turn 90° to the left into a left forward stance (apkubi, direction 4), and execute a low section block with the left arm (arae-makki).

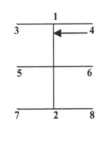

Keeping the right foot fixed, slide the left foot back and assume an open stance (oen-seogi). Execute simultaneouly a left hammer-fist downward strike (oen-mejumok-naeryo-chigi).

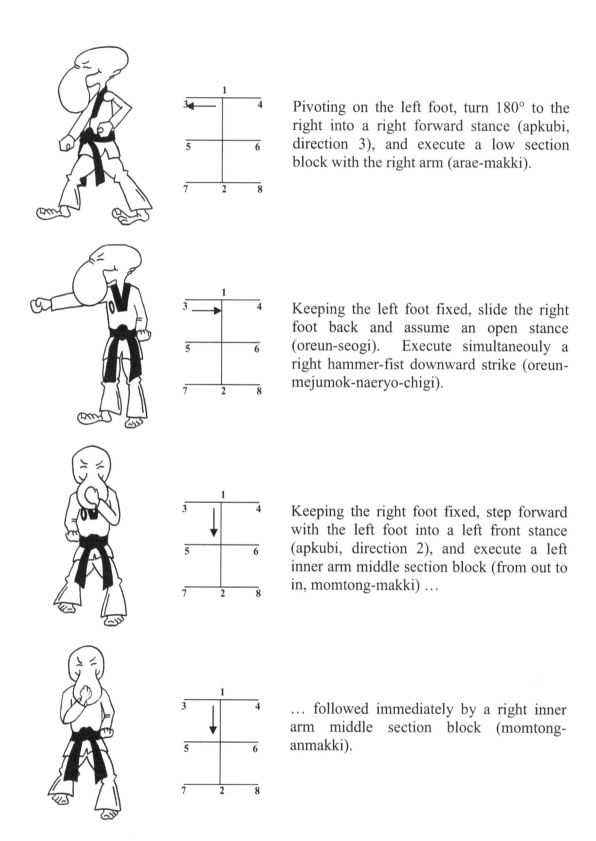

Pivoting on the left foot, turn 180° to the right into a right forward stance (apkubi, direction 3), and execute a low section block with the right arm (arae-makki).

Keeping the left foot fixed, slide the right foot back and assume an open stance (oreun-seogi). Execute simultaneouly a right hammer-fist downward strike (oreun-mejumok-naeryo-chigi).

Keeping the right foot fixed, step forward with the left foot into a left front stance (apkubi, direction 2), and execute a left inner arm middle section block (from out to in, momtong-makki) …

… followed immediately by a right inner arm middle section block (momtong-anmakki).

 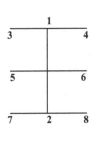

Keeping the left foot fixed, execute a front snap kick with the right foot (apchagi).

 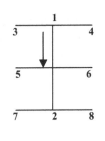

Step down into a right forward stance (apkubi, direction 2), and execute a right back fist strike to the face (oreun-deung-jumeok-ap-chigi) …

 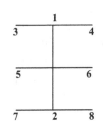

… followed immediately by a left middle section inner arm block (from out to in, momtong-anmakki).

 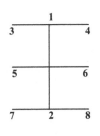

Keeping the right foot fixed, execute a front snap kick with the left foot (apchagi).

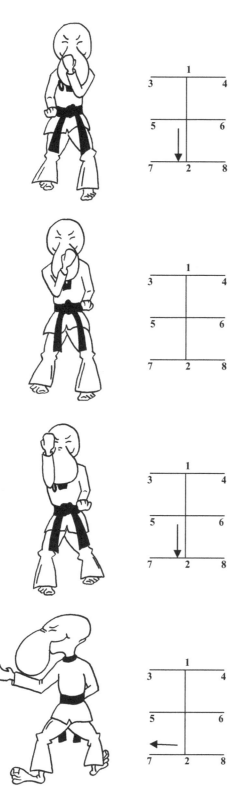

Step down into a left forward stance (apkubi, direction 2), and execute a left back fist strike to the face (oen-deung-jumeok-ap-chigi) …

… followed immediately by a right middle section inner arm block (from out to in, momtong-anmakki).

Keeping the left foot fixed, step forward into a right forward stance (apkubi), and execute a right back fist front strike to the face (oreun-deung-jumeok-ap-chigi).

Pivoting on the right foot, turn 270° to the left into a right back stance (oreun dwitkubi, direction 7), and execute a left knife-hand middle section outward block (from in to out, oen-hansonnal-bakkat-makki).

 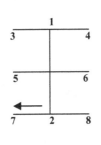 Keeping the left foot fixed, step forward with the right foot into a right forward stance (apkubi). At the same time cover the right fist with the left hand and execute a right elbow middle section strike (oreun-palgup-dollyo-chigi).

 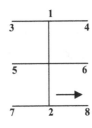 Pivoting on the left foot, turn 180° to the right into a left back stance (oen dwitkubi, direction 8), and execute a right knife-hand middle section outward block (from in to out, oreun-hansonnal-bakkat-makki).

 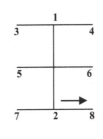 Keeping the right foot fixed, step forward with the left foot into a left forward stance (apkubi). At the same time cover the left fist with the right hand and execute a left elbow middle section strike (oen-palgup-dollyo-chigi).

 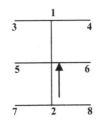 Pivoting on the right foot, turn 90° to the left (direction 1), into a left forward stance (apkubi), and execute a left low section block (arae-makki) …

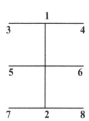

... followed by a right inner arm middle section block (from out to in, momtong-anmakki).

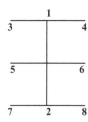

Keeping the left foot fixed, execute a right front snap kick (apchagi).

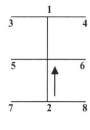

Step down with the right foot into a right forward stance (apkubi) and execute a right low section block (arae-makki)...

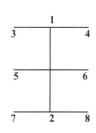

...followed by a left inner arm middle section block (from out to in, momtong-anmakki).

52

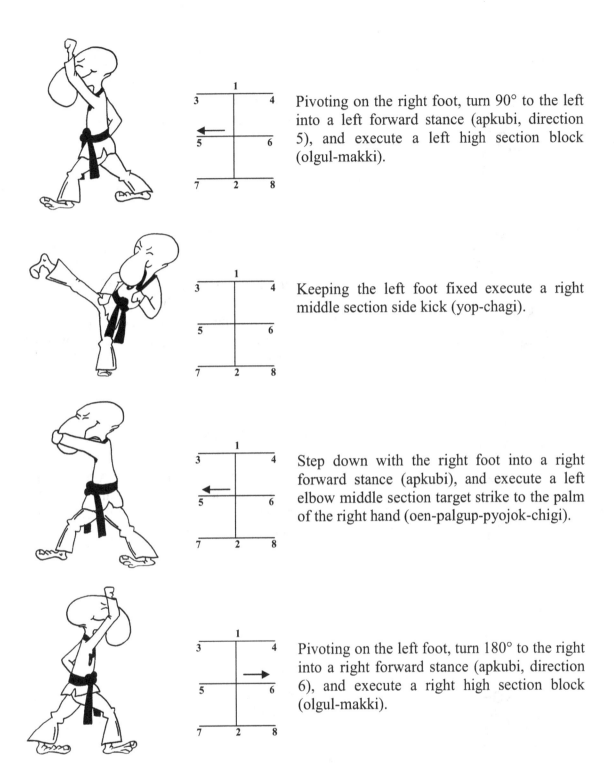

Pivoting on the right foot, turn 90° to the left into a left forward stance (apkubi, direction 5), and execute a left high section block (olgul-makki).

Keeping the left foot fixed execute a right middle section side kick (yop-chagi).

Step down with the right foot into a right forward stance (apkubi), and execute a left elbow middle section target strike to the palm of the right hand (oen-palgup-pyojok-chigi).

Pivoting on the left foot, turn 180° to the right into a right forward stance (apkubi, direction 6), and execute a right high section block (olgul-makki).

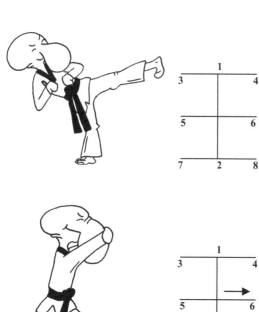

Keeping the right foot fixed execute a left middle sections side kick (yop-chagi).

Step down with the left foot into a left forward stance (apkubi), and execute a right elbow middle section target strike to the palm of the left hand (oreun-palgup-pyojok-chigi).

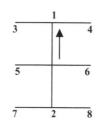

Pivoting on the right foot, turn 90° to the left into a left forward stance (apkubi, direction 1), and execute a left low section block (arae-makki) …

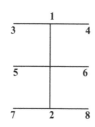

… followed by a right middle section inner arm block (from out to in, momtong-anmakki).

54

 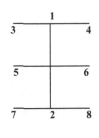

Execute a right front snap kick (apchagi) ...

 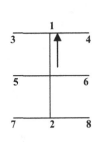

... without lowering the right foot, jump forward into a right twist stance (dwikkoa-seogi) and execute a right back fist front strike to the face (oreun-deungjumeok-ap-chigi).

KIHAPP!

55

TAEGUK YUK JANG

"BUG, 1995"

© Salma
Michor, VBK,
Vienna

56

TAEGUK 6 Jang

 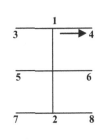

Pivoting on the right foot, turn 90° to the left into a left forward stance (apkubi, direction 4), and execute a low section block with the left arm (arae-makki).

 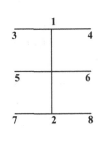

Keeping the left foot fixed, execute a right front snap kick (apchagi).

Step back with the right foot into a right back stance (oreun-dwitkubi), and execute a left outer arm middle section outward block (from in to out, momtong-bakkat-makki).

Pivoting on the left foot, turn 180° to the right into a right forward stance (apkubi, direction 3), and execute a low section block with the right arm (arae-makki).

Keeping the right foot fixed, execute a left front snap kick (apchagi).

Step back with the left foot into a left back stance (oen-dwitkubi), and execute a right outer arm middle section outward block (from in to out, momtong-bakkat-makki).

58

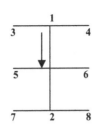

Pivoting on the right foot, turn 90° to the left into a left forward stance (apkubi, direction 2), and execute a right knife-hand high section outward block (from in to out, oreun-hansonnal-bitureo-makki).

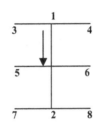

Pivoting on the left foot, execute a right high section turning kick (oreun-olgul-dollyo-chagi).

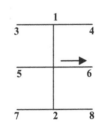

Step down with the right foot for a brief moment, and then step forward with the left foot into a left forward stance (apkubi). At the same time execute a left outer arm high section outward block (from in to out, olgul-bakkat-makki) …

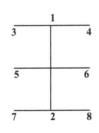

… followed immediately by a right fist straight punch to the middle section (momtong-baro-jireugi).

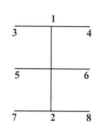

Keeping the left foot fixed, execute a front snap kick with the right foot (apchagi).

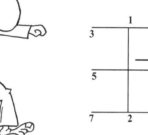

Step down into a right forward stance (apkubi, direction 6), and execute a left fist straight punch to the middle section (momtong-baro-jireugi).

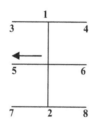

Pivoting on the left foot, turn 180° to the right into a right forward stance (apkubi, direction 5), and execute a right outer arm high section outward block (from in to out, olgul-bakkat-makki) ...

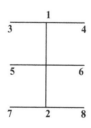

... followed immediately by a left fist straight punch to the middle section (momtong-baro-jireugi).

60

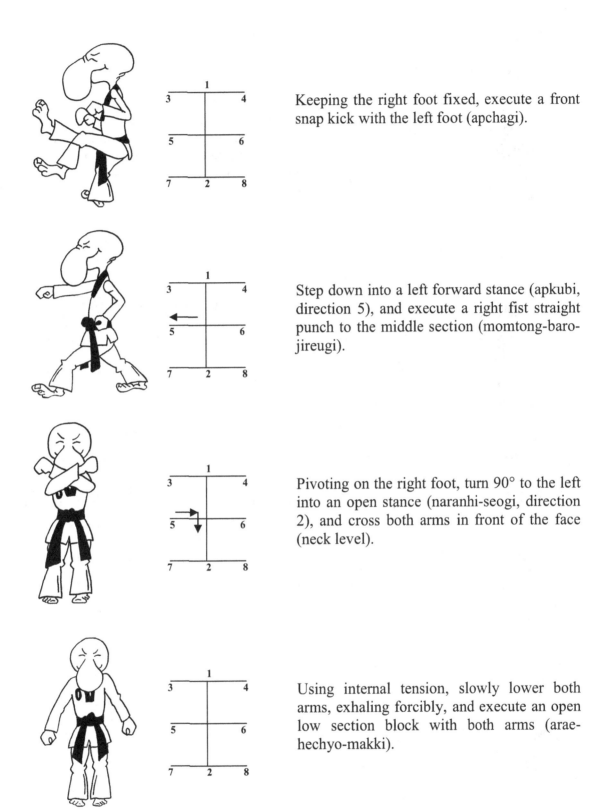

Keeping the right foot fixed, execute a front snap kick with the left foot (apchagi).

Step down into a left forward stance (apkubi, direction 5), and execute a right fist straight punch to the middle section (momtong-baro-jireugi).

Pivoting on the right foot, turn 90° to the left into an open stance (naranhi-seogi, direction 2), and cross both arms in front of the face (neck level).

Using internal tension, slowly lower both arms, exhaling forcibly, and execute an open low section block with both arms (arae-hechyo-makki).

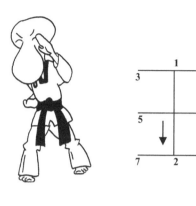

Keeping the left foot fixed, step forward with the right foot into a right forward stance (apkubi, direction 2), and execute a knife-hand high section outward block with the left hand (from in to out, oen-hansonnal- bitureo-makki).

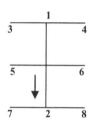

Keeping the right foot fixed, execute a left high section turning kick (oen-olgul-dollyo-chagi).

KIHAPP!

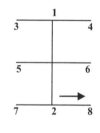

Step down, then pivot on the left foot and turn 270° to the right. Assume a right forward stance (apkubi, direction 8), and execute a low section block with the right arm (arae-makki).

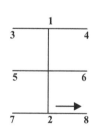

Keeping the right foot fixed, execute a front snap kick with the left foot (apchagi).

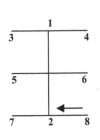

Step back into a left back stance (oen-dwitkubi) and execute a right outer arm middle section outward block (from in to out, momtong-bakkat-makki).

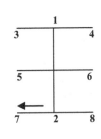

Pivoting on the right foot, turn 180° to the left into a left forward stance (apkubi, direction 7), and execute a low section block with the left arm (arae-makki).

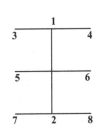

Keeping the left foot fixed, execute a right front snap kick (apchagi).

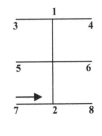

Step back into a right back stance (oreun-dwitkubi), and execute a left outer arm middle section outward block (from in to out, momtong-bakkat-makki).

63

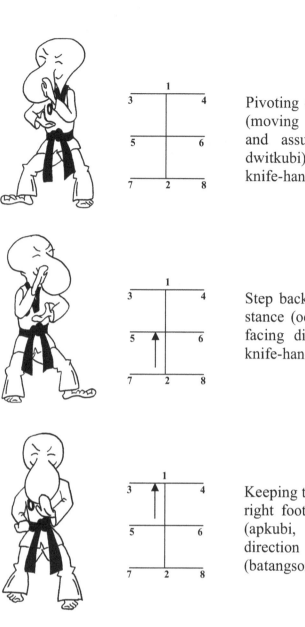

Pivoting on the left foot, turn 90° to the left (moving in direction 1, facing direction 2), and assume a right back stance (oreun dwitkubi). At the same time execute a double knife-hand block (sonnal-momtong-makki).

Step back with the left foot, into a left back stance (oen-dwitkubi, moving in direction 1, facing direction 2), and execute a double knife-hand block (sonnal-momtong-makki).

Keeping the left foot fixed, step back with the right foot and assume a left forward stance (apkubi, moving in direction 1, facing direction 2), and execute a left palm block (batangson-momtong-makki)…

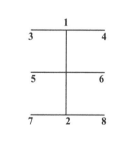

… in the same position, execute quickly a right middle section straight punch (momtong-baro-jireugi).

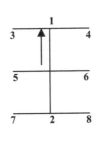

Keeping the right foot fixed, step back with the left foot and assume a right forward stance (apkubi, moving in direction 1, facing direction 2), and execute a right palm block (batangson-momtong-makki) ...

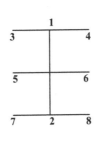

... followed by a left middle section straight punch (momtong-baro-jireugi).

TAEGUK CHIL JANG

"BUG, 1995"

© Salma
Michor, VBK,
Vienna

TAEGUK 7 Jang

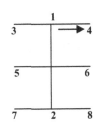

Pivoting on the right foot, turn 90° to the left into a left tiger stance (oen-bomseogi, direction 4), and execute a right middle section palm block (batangson-momtong-anmakki).

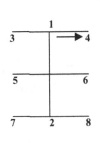

Keeping the left foot fixed, execute a right front sanp kick (apchagi).

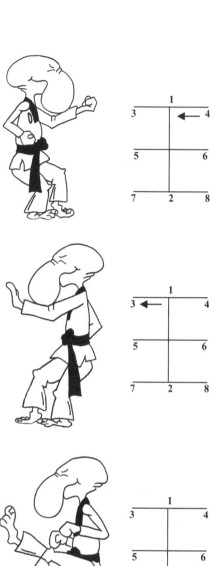

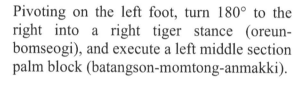

Step back into a left tiger stance (oen-bomseogi) and execute a left inner arm block (from out to in, momtong-makki).

Pivoting on the left foot, turn 180° to the right into a right tiger stance (oreun-bomseogi), and execute a left middle section palm block (batangson-momtong-anmakki).

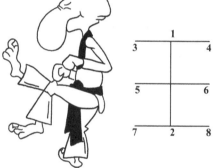

Keeping the right foot fixed, execute a left front sanp kick (apchagi).

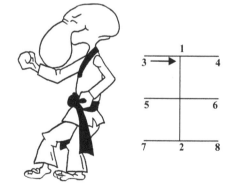

Step back into a right tiger stance (oreun-bomseogi) and execute a right inner arm block (from out to in, momtong-makki).

 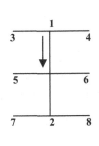

Pivoting on the right foot, turn 90° to the left into a right back stance (oreun-dwitkubi), and execute a left double knife-hand low section block (sonnal-arae-makki).

 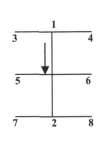

Keeping the left foot fixed, step forward into a left back stance and execute and execute a right double knife-hand low section block (sonnal-arae-makki).

 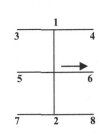

Pivoting on the right foot, turn 90° to the left into a left tiger stance (oen-bomseogi), and execute a right palm block. At the same time move the left fist under the right elbow (batangson-momtong-guduro-anmakki).

 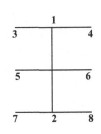

In the same position, and keeping the left fist under the right elbow, execute quickly a right high section back fist strike (oreun-deungjumeok-olgul-ap-chigi).

69

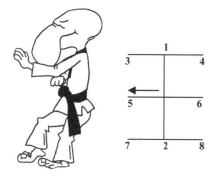

Turn 180° to the right into a right tiger stance (oreun-bomseogi), and execute a left palm block. At the same time move the right fist under the left elbow (batangson-momtong-guduro-anmakki).

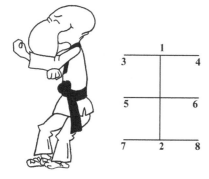

In the same position, and keeping the right fist under the left elbow, execute quickly a left high section back fist strike (oen-deungjumeok-olgul-ap-chigi).

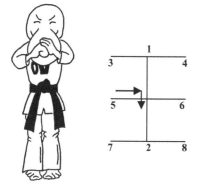

Pivoting on the left foot, turn 90° to the left (direction 2), while moving the right foot beside the left, and assume a closed stance (moa-seogi). Make a fist with the right hand and cover it with the left palm. Bring both hands up slowly to chin level (bo-jumeok).

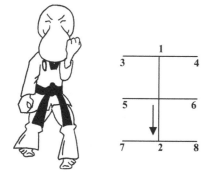

Keeping the right foot fixed, step forward with the left foot into a left forward stance (apkubi) and execute simultaneously a left outer arm block and a right low section block (oen-palmok-momtong-makki and oreun-palmok-arae-makki = gawi-makki) ...

 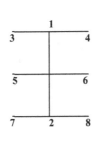 ... followed by a right outer arm block and a left low section block (scissors block, dubon-gawi-makki).

 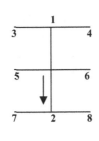 Keeping the left foot fixed, step forward with the right foot into a right forward stance (apkubi) and execute simultaneously a right outer arm block and a left low section block (oreun-palmok-momtong-makki and oen palmok-arae-makki = gawi-makki) ...

 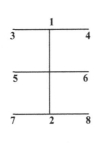 ... followed by a left outer arm block and a right low section block (scissors block, dubon-gawi-makki).

 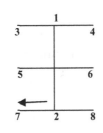 Pivoting on the right foot, turn 270° to the left and assume a left forward stance (apkubi). At the same time execute an outer arm middle section block with both arms (momtong-hechyo-makki).

71

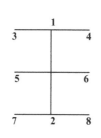

Execute a right knee middle section strike (oreun-mureup-chigi).

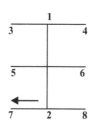

Jump forward into a twist stance (dwikkoa-seogi) and execute quickly a double fist middle section upper cut knuckle punch with both hands (dojumeok-techeo-jireugi).

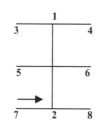

Keeping the right foot fixed, step back with the left foot and assume a right forward stance (apkubi). At the same time execute a cross wrist low section block (otgeoreo-arae-makki).

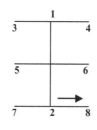

Pivoting on the left foot, turn 180° to the right and assume a right forward stance (apkubi). At the same time execute an outer arm middle section block with both arms (momtong-hechyo-makki).

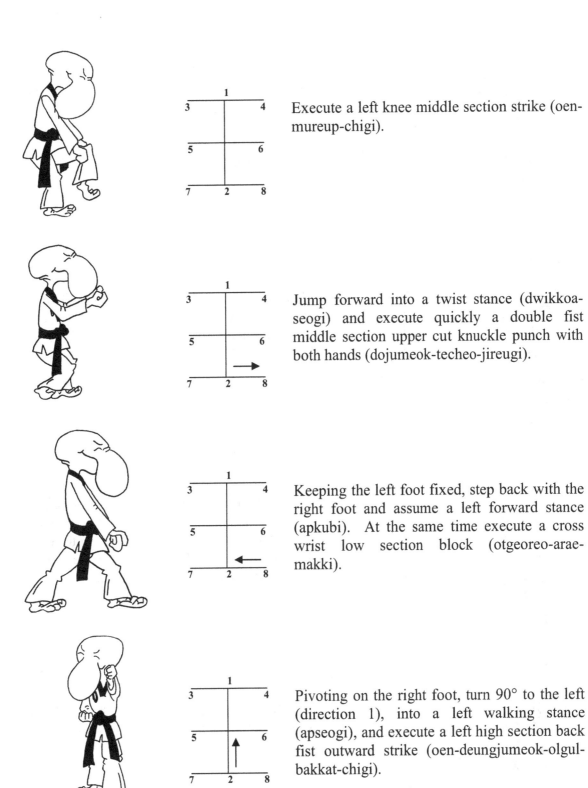

Execute a left knee middle section strike (oen-mureup-chigi).

Jump forward into a twist stance (dwikkoa-seogi) and execute quickly a double fist middle section upper cut knuckle punch with both hands (dojumeok-techeo-jireugi).

Keeping the left foot fixed, step back with the right foot and assume a left forward stance (apkubi). At the same time execute a cross wrist low section block (otgeoreo-arae-makki).

Pivoting on the right foot, turn 90° to the left (direction 1), into a left walking stance (apseogi), and execute a left high section back fist outward strike (oen-deungjumeok-olgul-bakkat-chigi).

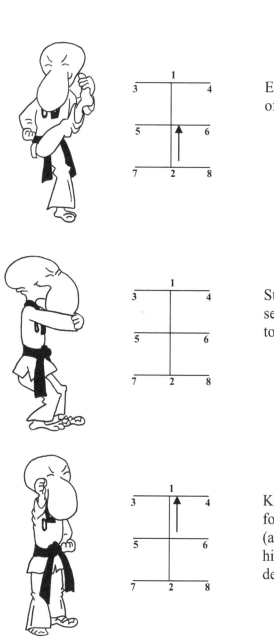

Execute a right inner crescent kick to the palm of the left hand (oreun-pyojeok-chagi).

Step down into a horse riding stance (juchum-seogi), and execute a right elbow target strike to the left palm (oreun-palgup-pyojeok-chigi).

Keeping the right foot fixed, slide the left foot forward and assume a right walking stance (apseogi). At the same time execute a right high section back fist outward strike (oreun-deungjumeok-olgul-bakkat-chigi).

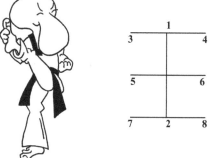

Execute a left inner crescent kick to the palm of the right hand (oen-pyojeok-chagi).

74

 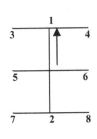

Step down into a horse riding stance (juchum-seogi), and execute a left elbow target strike to the right palm (oen-palgup-pyojeok-chigi).

 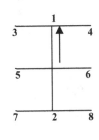

In the same position, execute a left middle section knife-hand outward block (from in to out, oen-hannsonal-momtong-yop-makki).

 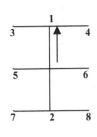

Pivoting on the left foot, move the right foot forward and assume a horse riding stance (juchum seogi). At the same time execute a right middle section side punch (oreun-momtong-yop-jireugi).

KIHAPP!

TAEGUK PAL JANG

"BUG, 1995"

76

TAEGUK 8 Jang

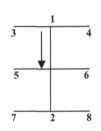

Step forward with the left foot into a right back stance (oreun-dwitkubi, direction 2), and execute a left outer arm block (geodeureo-bakkat-makki). The right arm gaurds the solar plexus.

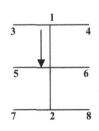

Slide forward with the left foot into a long stance (apkubi) and execute a right middle section punch (momtong-baro-jireugi).

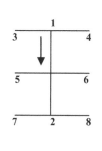

Leap into the air and execute a twin jump kick (dobal-dangsong-ap-chagi).

KIHAPP!

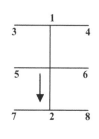

Land in a left long stance (oen-apkubi), and execute a left outer arm inside block (from out to in, momtong-makki) …

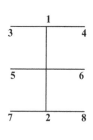

…followed by a right …

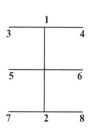

…and then a left straight punch in rapid succession (momtong-dubeon-jireugi).

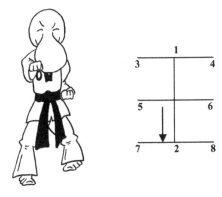

Step forward with the right foot into a long stance (apkubi, direction 2), and execute a right middle section reverse punch (momtong-bandae-jireugi).

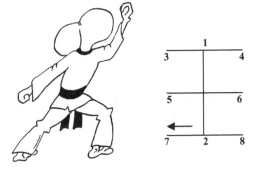

Pivoting on the right foot, turn 270° to the left (direction 7) in a right long stance (oreun-apkubi) while executing a right high section outer arm block and a left low section block (owesanteul-makki).

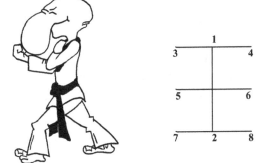

In the same position, twist the body to the left into a left forward stance (oen-apkubi, direction 7) and execute a right upper-cut punch while bringing the left fist to the shoulder (oreun-danggyo-tok-jireugi).

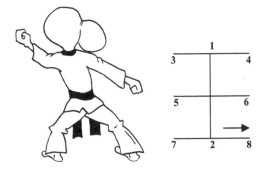

Step across with the left foot temporarily into a left X-stance (direction 8), then step with the right foot into a left long stance (apkubi). At the same time execute a left outer arm high section block and a right low section block (owesanteul-makki).

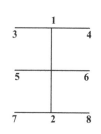

In the same position, twist the body to the right into a right forward stance (oreun-apkubi, direction 8) and execute a left upper-cut punch while bringing the right fist to the shoulder (oen-danggyo-tok-jireugi).

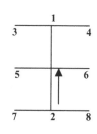

Turn 90° to the left (moving in direction 1, facing direction 2) into a right back stance (oreun-dwitkubi). At the same time execute a double knife-hand block (oen-sonnal-momtong-makki).

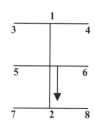

Slide forward into a left forward stance (apkubi, direction 2) and execute quickly a right middle section reverse punch (momtong-baro-jireugi).

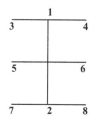

Execute a right middle section front snap kick (apchagi).

80

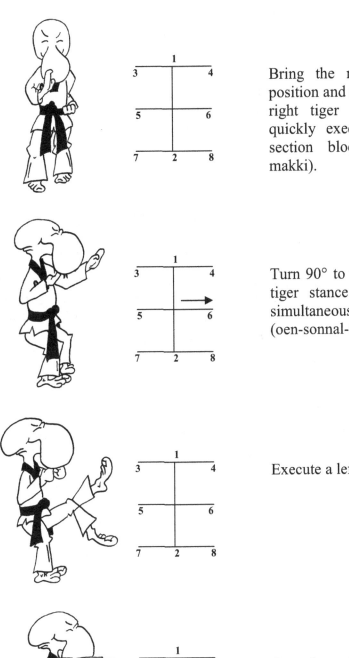

Bring the right foot back to the initial position and step back with the left foot into a right tiger stance (oreun-boomseogi) and quickly execute a right palm fist middle section block (oreun-batangson-momtong-makki).

Turn 90° to the right (direction 6) into a left tiger stance (oen-boomseogi) and execute simultaneously a left double knife-hand block (oen-sonnal-momtong-makki).

Execute a left front snap kick (apchagi).

Step down into a left forward stance (oen-apkubi) and execute quickly a right middle section reverse punch (momtong-baro-jireugi).

81

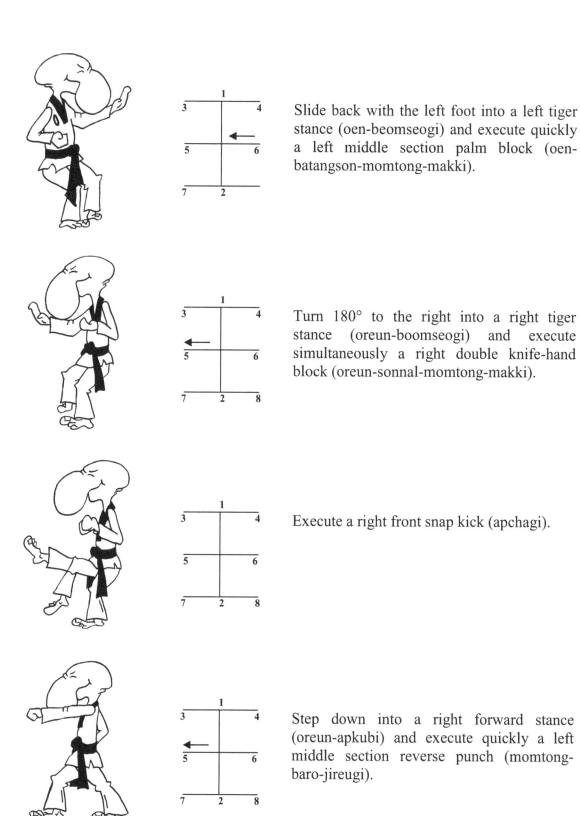

Slide back with the left foot into a left tiger stance (oen-beomseogi) and execute quickly a left middle section palm block (oen-batangson-momtong-makki).

Turn 180° to the right into a right tiger stance (oreun-boomseogi) and execute simultaneously a right double knife-hand block (oreun-sonnal-momtong-makki).

Execute a right front snap kick (apchagi).

Step down into a right forward stance (oreun-apkubi) and execute quickly a left middle section reverse punch (momtong-baro-jireugi).

 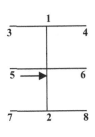 Slide back with the right foot into a right tiger stance (oreun-beomseogi) and execute quickly a right middle section palm block (oreun-batangson-momtong-makki).

 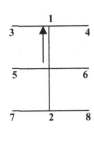 Turn 90° to the right (direction 1) into a left back stance (oen-dwitkubi) and execute simultaneously a right low section block while the left fist guards the solar plexus (geodeureo-arae-makki).

 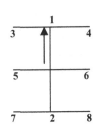 Execute a left front snap kick (apchagi).

 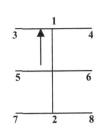 Leap in the air and execute a right jump front snap kick (apchagi).

KIHAPP!

83

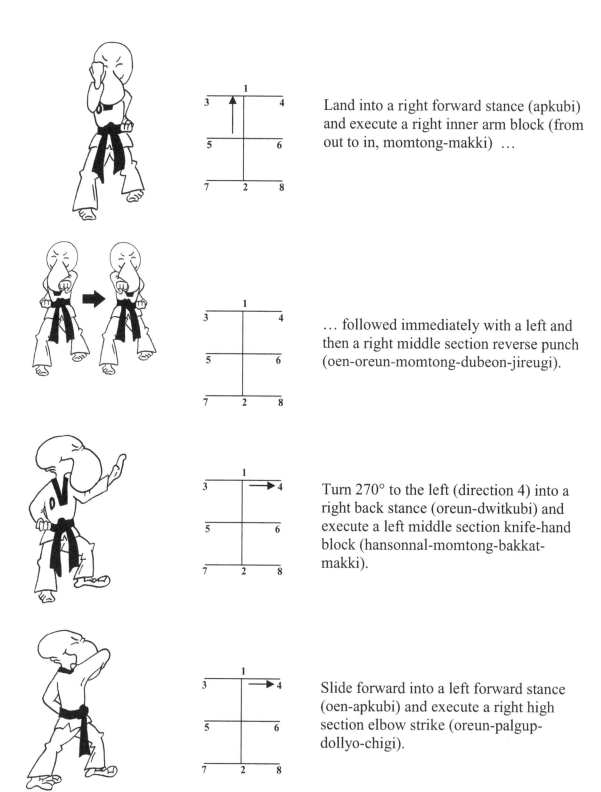

Land into a right forward stance (apkubi) and execute a right inner arm block (from out to in, momtong-makki) …

… followed immediately with a left and then a right middle section reverse punch (oen-oreun-momtong-dubeon-jireugi).

Turn 270° to the left (direction 4) into a right back stance (oreun-dwitkubi) and execute a left middle section knife-hand block (hansonnal-momtong-bakkat-makki).

Slide forward into a left forward stance (oen-apkubi) and execute a right high section elbow strike (oreun-palgup-dollyo-chigi).

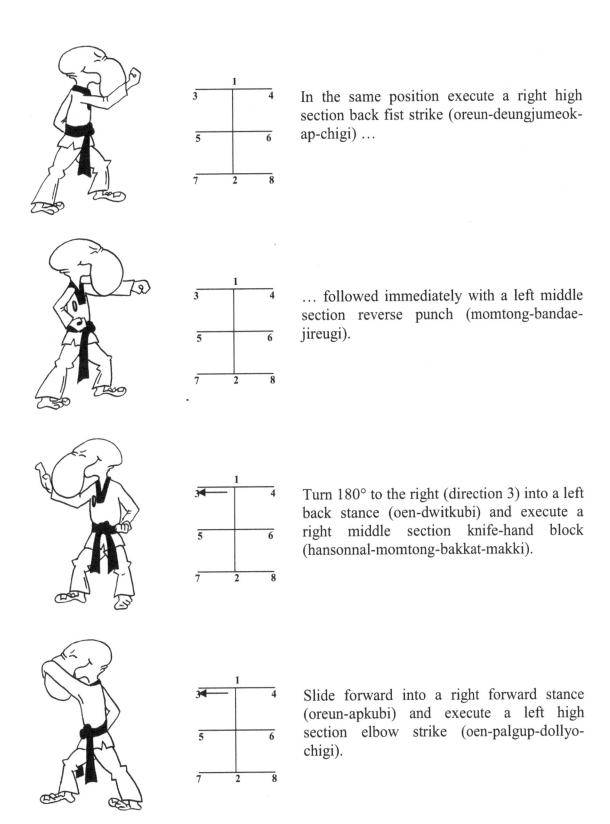

In the same position execute a right high section back fist strike (oreun-deungjumeok-ap-chigi) …

… followed immediately with a left middle section reverse punch (momtong-bandae-jireugi).

Turn 180° to the right (direction 3) into a left back stance (oen-dwitkubi) and execute a right middle section knife-hand block (hansonnal-momtong-bakkat-makki).

Slide forward into a right forward stance (oreun-apkubi) and execute a left high section elbow strike (oen-palgup-dollyo-chigi).

85

 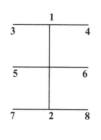 In the same position execute a left high section back fist strike (oen-deungjumeok-ap-chigi) …

 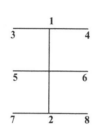 … followed immediately with a right middle section reverse punch (momtong-bandae-jireugi).

86

EPILOGUE

After many long years of hard training, the Bug became an experienced and capable taekwondo fighter and trainer. The Bug took part in numerous national and international tournaments and never lost a fight to anyone. The Bug could now not only kick and punch in all directions but it could also change its form!!!!

As a taekwondo master, the Bug decided to open its own martial arts school and now gives lessons for children and adults and never ceases to impress the young and old alike!

LITERATURE

1. Cho, Hee Il: The Complete Tae Geuk Hyung, WTF, USA, 1988.

2. Kim, Jeong Rok: Taekwondo, Basic Techniques & Taeguek poomse, Vol. I., Seo Lim P.Co., Korea, 1986.

3. Kukkiwon: Taekwondo Textbook. Kukkiwon Ed. Korea, O-Sung Publishing Co. 1997.

4. Lee, Kyong Myong: Richtig Taekwondo (Die Kunst der Unbewaffneten Selbstverteidigung), 1987.

5. Yeon, Hee Park: Yeon, Hwan Park, Jon Gerrad: Taekwondo, The Ultimate Reference Guide to the World's Most popular Martial Art. Facts on file, Inc. USA 1989.

6. Ikpil, Kang / Namjung Song: The Explanation of official Taekwondo Poomse, Sang-A Publishing Company, 2008.